MODERN ERAS · UNCOVERED

the mid 1940s to the early 1960s

From Television to the Berlin Wall

Pat Levy

Raintree

Chicago, Illinois

© 2006 Raintree
Published by Raintree
A division of Reed Elsevier, Inc.
Chicago, IL

For information, address the publisher:
Raintree, 100 N. LaSalle, Suite 1200
Chicago, IL 60602
Customer Service: 888-363-4266
Visit our website at www.raintreelibrary.com

Printed and bound in China by South China
Printing Company

10 09 08 07 06
10 9 8 7 6 5 4 3 2 1

**Library of Congress Cataloging-in-
Publication Data**
Sheehan, Sean, 1951-
  From television to the Berlin Wall : the mid-
1940s to the early 1960s / Sean Sheehan.
     p. cm. -- (Modern eras uncovered)
  Includes index.
  ISBN 1-41091-787-8 (library binding-
hardcover) -- ISBN 1-41091-796-7 (pbk.)
  1. History, Modern--1945-1989--Juvenile
literature. 2. Civilization, Modern--20th
century--Juvenile literature. I. Title. II. Series.
  D842.5.S55 2005
  909.82'5--dc22
                              2005002409

Acknowledgments
Corbis p. 22; Corbis/Bettmann pp. 4, 5, 7,
17, 20, 26, 27, 34, 35, 38, 44, 49 (top);
Corbis/Hulton Deutsch Collection pp. 24,
37; Corbis/Pablo Corral Vega p. 39;
Corbis/Roger Ressmeyer p. 41; Corbis/Terry
Cryer p. 45; Getty Images/Hulton Archive
pp. 11, 12, 13, 21, 23, 25, 32, 33, 36, 42, 43,
47; Getty Images/Time Life Pictures pp. 6,
31, 46, 49 (bottom); The Advertising Archive
Ltd pp. 10, 14, 15, 40; The Bridgeman Art
Library/Private Collection p. 30; The Novosti
Press Agency pp. 28, 29

Cover photographs (top and bottom)
reproduced with permission of Corbis.

CONTENTS

Any words appearing in the text in bold, **like this,** are explained in the glossary.

A POSTWAR WORLD

World War II ended in 1945. It had been a total war, meaning it involved nearly every country in the world. For the first time, more ordinary **civilians** had died than soldiers. There had been terrible acts of racial hatred during the war, and when it was over, people all over the world had to address these harsh realities.

The war had destroyed whole cities and millions of homes all over the world. Many European countries had lost much of their wealth. Food was in short supply, especially in the **USSR**. Only in the United States, where war never reached the continental borders, did people's incomes rise and the **economy** grow stronger as a result of the war.

Germany and Japan had lost the war, and so they were no longer leading world powers. The United States and the USSR were now the new world leaders. They had been allies during the war, but this friendship quickly ended. Their leaders had different ideas about the best way to organize society. This developed into a new kind of war called a **Cold War**, in which both countries developed huge stores of **nuclear** weapons, but never actually used them.

After the war, African Americans in the United States demanded full **civil rights**. Meanwhile, former **empires** such as the United Kingdom saw their **colonies** in Asia and Africa demand independence.

A U.S. Navy officer greets his wife and daughters on a dock in California after returning from duty in the Pacific.

The hard times of war began to ease by the late 1950s, when people began to feel confident about the future. New technologies were improving the quality of life, and young people enjoyed wealth that their parents had never known as teenagers.

The technology of television signaled a new world, but the building of the **Berlin Wall** in 1961 was a product of the Cold War. People growing up in this period had good reason to feel hopeful, but they also had reason to be fearful.

American women enjoy the new products of the 1950s as they shop in Gimbel's department store in New York.

Tears and laughter

A woman, traveling to meet her soldier husband, remembers hearing news of the end of the war in a railroad station:

"An old lady beside me burst out crying. I did the same, a soldier whom I did not know picked me up and swung me around, the spare engine standing in the station just sounded its horn for a full five minutes, everyone spoke to everyone else, we were all so happy."

(FROM *HOW WE LIVED THEN* BY NORMAN LONGMAN)

THE AFTERMATH OF WAR

After the trauma and suffering caused by the **Great Depression** and World War II, many Americans, especially veterans, aspired to stability and normality. After the 1944 GI Bill of Rights was passed, the U.S. government agreed to pay any educational costs for veterans. This allowed more Americans from lower and middle social classes to get college educations than ever before. These educational possibilities, combined with the United States' rapidly improving economy, set the stage for a period of great prosperity among this generation of Americans.

Picking up the pieces

Around the world, people began to try to get their lives back to normal. There were about 40 million homeless people in China as a result of the war against Japanese occupation. Food was in short supply everywhere, and in some countries people were starving. In the United States, over 120,000 Japanese-Americans had been forced to move into **detention camps** when the war began. These camps were poorly built, fenced barracks guarded by armed soldiers. When the prisoners were released from the camps at the end of the war, many found they had lost their homes and possessions because they could not afford to make their payments while inside the camps. In Japan itself, people faced the effects of two **atomic bombs** dropped on the cities of Hiroshima and Nagasaki.

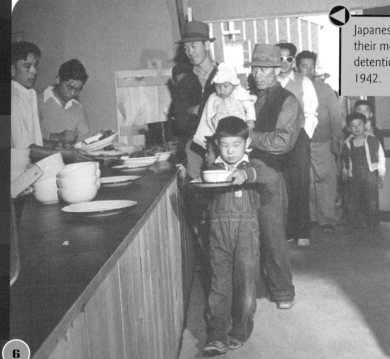

Japanese-Americans line up for their meals at Heart Mountain detention camp, Wyoming, in 1942.

"We don't want you here!"

Victor Breitburg was a Jew who survived the **Holocaust** and returned to his home in Poland after the war:

"I saw a man who was still wearing the stripes [striped prison clothes] from the concentration camp. As I tried to approach him, two Polish people started to question him. 'Hey, Jew, where are you going? . . . We don't want you here!' I was dumbfounded . . . I felt like shouting at them: 'You didn't help us; you turned us in; you are worse than the Germans.'" (FROM *NEVER AGAIN* BY MARTIN GILBERT)

Deportations

In the USSR, people the government thought had not supported them during the war were forced to go to labor camps called **gulags**. Also forced into these camps were whole communities that belonged to **ethnic minorities**. In all, about 15 to 30 million **Soviet** citizens died in the gulags.

Across Europe there were millions of **refugees**. In Germany alone there were nine million refugees, called **displaced persons** (DPs). Some were people who the Nazis had **deported** from their home countries to work as slave laborers in Germany. Others were citizens of countries in eastern Europe. They had fled into Germany when Soviet soldiers began invading from the east toward the end of the war. Others were Jews rescued from the German **concentration camps**. After the war, these camps were used to house DPs. Many DPs, helped by emigration plans, moved abroad to Canada, the United States, Australia, and South America.

The SS *Marine Flasher* arrives in New York, May 20, 1946, carrying over 800 displaced persons admitted to the United States after the war. Many were orphans whose parents were lost in the war or in Nazi concentration camps.

Nations United?

During the war, U.S. President Franklin D. Roosevelt had referred to the **Allied powers** (the United States, the USSR, the United Kingdom, France, and China) as the **United Nations**. In April 1945 a conference was held to establish a new world organization. The United Nations (UN) was made into an official assembly, and these countries became full members.

Dividing up the world

In public, the Allied powers all supported a **democratic** world in which countries decided their own futures. In private, they made agreements about who would influence the rest of Europe. Europe was roughly divided so that countries in the east came under Soviet **communist** influence while countries in the west came under Western **capitalist** influence.

The United States, USSR, United Kingdom, and France divided Germany into four zones, with each country governing its own zone. The capital city of Berlin, which was located in the Soviet zone, was itself divided up into four sectors (see map below).

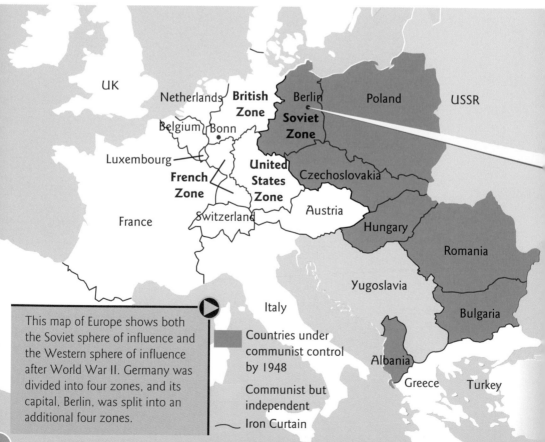

This map of Europe shows both the Soviet sphere of influence and the Western sphere of influence after World War II. Germany was divided into four zones, and its capital, Berlin, was split into an additional four zones.

Countries under communist control by 1948

Communist but independent

Iron Curtain

Capitalist vs. communist

The United States feared the system of communism, which the USSR supported. The USSR feared the system of capitalism, which the United States supported. In 1945 the United States was the only country able to put money into the reconstruction of a war-wrecked Europe. The Marshall Plan, named after U.S. Secretary of State George C. Marshall, pumped billions of dollars into western Europe. The aim was to speed up economic growth, settle down the political problems, and weaken the appeal of communist parties to western European citizens.

The USSR refused money from the United States, and it used its enormous political influence to make sure countries in eastern Europe also refused. The Marshall Plan was seen by the USSR as an attempt by the United States to weaken the USSR's power and the communist system. Europe became firmly divided between communist and capitalist powers. Britain's wartime leader, Winston Churchill, spoke of an "Iron Curtain" dividing the two.

Different points of view

In 1948 the United States supported introducing a new currency called the Deutschmark into the western half of Germany. The USSR, which did not want this western currency being used in Berlin, stopped supplies of food and other goods from traveling through eastern Germany to reach the western half of Berlin. The United States responded by flying in supplies by airplane until the **blockade** was lifted. This was called the Berlin airlift. From one point of view, the USSR was acting aggressively against West Berlin. From another, the U.S.- backed new currency was an attempt to bring all of Berlin into a capitalist system.

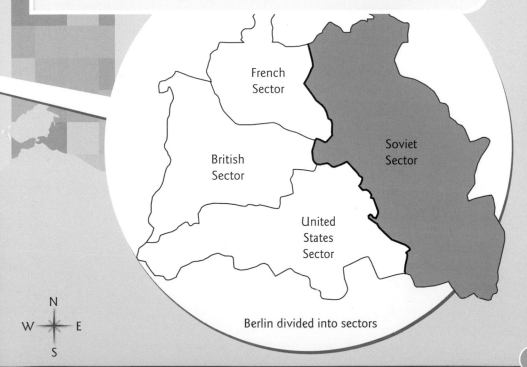

French
Sector

Soviet
Sector

British
Sector

United
States
Sector

N
W — E
S

Berlin divided into sectors

Television replaced radio in popularity during the postwar period. Popular TV formats included variety shows (such as *The Ed Sullivan Show*), soap operas, children's shows (such as *The Howdy Doody Show*), news, comedies (such as *I Love Lucy* and *The Honeymooners*), and westerns (such as *Gunsmoke*). However, family comedies, such as *Leave It to Beaver*, *Lassie*, and *The Adventures of Ozzie and Harriet*, perhaps best embodied the period. These programs presented the notion of a wholesome, perfect American family that many people still associate with the 1950s.

Radio

Radio had been an important part of the lives of millions of people during the war. Wartime radios had been large pieces of wooden furniture. With the invention of **transistors**, radios became small, lightweight objects that could be carried around the house. Sound quality improved enormously and stereo was introduced. Radio shows in the United States included sitcoms such as *Life with Luigi*, a story about an **immigrant** family, westerns such as the *Lone Ranger*, music broadcasts, and regular news programs.

▲ This advertisement shows some of the electrical appliances available during the 1950s, including refrigerators and stoves.

Television

When World War II ended, television was in its early stages of development. Television programming had begun before the war, but there was only a tiny audience. In the late 1940s and early 1950s, radio stars such as Bob Hope, Jack Benny, and Milton Berle moved their radio shows to television, which helped bring large audiences to the new, unfamiliar medium.

The first color broadcast was made in 1951, and by 1954 broadcasts were regularly in color. By 1958 50 million people in the United States, 31 percent of the population, owned a television set. By the early 1960s, over 90 percent of U.S. homes had a television set.

Consumer boom

By the 1950s, **consumer goods** were flooding onto the market for ordinary people to buy. The German-designed, rechargeable Braun electric razor came out in 1954. Vacuum cleaners became cheap and popular, and Earl Tupper developed a popular system of plastic storage tubs called Tupperware. These were ideal for storing food in refrigerators, which more and more families could afford. **Thermoplastics** changed the design of thousands of everyday items, since it allowed them be molded into different shapes.

Quiz show scandals

In the 1950s, quiz shows were popular prime-time television programs. Millions of Americans watched them. Contestants played for thousands of dollars, and if successful one week, they returned the next week to risk their winnings once more. In 1958 a scandal broke out when former contestants began to admit that they had been given answers to the questions. It turned out that the shows had given answers to the contestants that the audience liked and let the unpopular ones lose. That year, **Congress** passed a law making the fixing of a television game show a crime.

▲ Television host Hal March questions a contestant inside the booth during the television quiz show *The $64,000 Question* in 1955.

New Fashions

During World War II, there had been serious shortages of clothes in the countries involved in the war. Silk had been needed for parachutes, factories were needed for making uniforms and weapons, and workers were needed for fighting. Women's magazines of the time encouraged women to make over their dresses from the previous year. Since silk was in short supply, most women could not buy silk stockings. Some women drew black lines up the backs of their bare legs to imitate the look of the seams on the stockings of the day.

The New Look

In the Europe, the hardships of the war continued into the 1950s, but in 1947 the French designer Christian Dior changed women's fashions completely. Instead of practical suits and sensible skirts, Dior's models had narrow waists and long, full skirts using huge amounts of cloth. They were expensive and luxurious. The look was meant to be a change from the clothes of hardship. Dior's designs were only available to the very wealthy, but more affordable brands began to copy them almost immediately. Another French designer, Hubert de Givenchy, became known for his elegant designs for the actress Audrey Hepburn.

A model shows off a luxurious black velvet evening gown from the new collection at Christian Dior, Paris, France, in August 1953.

Make do and mend

Dior's designs were meant for the small number of women with enough money to spend on expensive designer clothes. Ordinary women tried to adapt the clothes they had to the new styles. One woman remembered making a Dior-style skirt out of old "blackout" material. This was the cheap cloth that people in the UK placed over their windows to stop German bombers from using a house's lights to help them identify targets.

Public reactions

In New York, some women protested against the New Look as an unnecessary waste of money and a setback in the fight for women's equality with men. In the United Kingdom, politicians discussed the cost to the economy that the manufacture of such expensive clothes would involve. An even bigger fashion revolution came in 1946, when the bikini, named after the island on which the first atomic bomb tests were made, became available.

Department stores

Nylon stockings went on sale in May 1940 in the United States and sold out in four days. Before this, stockings had been made of silk, which was very expensive, or wool, which was very rough. Nylon was cheap, washed well, did not fade, and could be mixed with natural fibers. It began to be used for a whole range of clothing. Suddenly, department stores such as Macy's and J.C. Penny sold affordable and attractive clothing that ordinary women had never been able to acquire before. By the late 1950s, these department stores had 50 million customers a week. British stores such as Marks and Spencer also thrived.

Crowds of shoppers swarm the checkout aisle inside a large Marks and Spencer store in the UK, November 1955.

Cars and Planes

During the war, gasoline had been **rationed** in many countries. Cars often were kept in garages until the end of the war. In the United States, rationing ended very soon after the war's end. There, as part of the boom in demand for consumer goods, the car industry exploded. Cars became much more than a way of getting from one place to another. They represented wealth and the freedom of the "open road." Cars grew ever bigger, shinier, and faster, with chrome fins and bumpers, big headlights, and a shiny grille on the front. Advertisements suggested that the owners of cars such as the Studebaker, Ford, or Mercury were more glamorous and wealthy than people who still used prewar models. The big, bold style of these cars came to represent the American spirit during this period.

European cars

In Europe, cars tended to be smaller and more fuel-efficient. In the United Kingdom, the "bubble car" was invented—a tiny three-wheeled car with a front opening hatch. In Germany, the Messerschmitt Cabin Scooter of 1953 was a cross between a motorcycle and a car. In Italy, a company developed the Vespa scooter, a motorcycle with a tiny gasoline engine and a top speed of 50 miles (80 kilometers) per hour. It and its rival, the Lambretta, became enormously popular in western Europe because they were both so stylish.

An exciting eyeful and amazingly thrifty!

Studebaker Starliner

AMERICA'S SMARTEST "HARD-TOP"

'52 Studebaker

The new, stylish Studebaker Starliner car represented wealth and prosperity in the 1950s in the United States.

Commercial jets

The first commercial jet airliner flew in May 1952 when BOAC (British Overseas Airways Corporation) flew a jet from London to Johannesburg in South Africa. In 1957 the Boeing 707 jet airplane went into service in the United States. It could carry 180 passengers and signaled the end of the age of great passenger ships.

In the air

Air transportation had been in development before the war. European countries had formed national airlines and built small airports near capital cities. Such developments were abandoned during the war, when all design and manufacture went into fighter planes. After the war, the airports returned, and passenger airplanes were built with jet engines. Their lighter bodies gave faster speeds for less fuel, while wing flaps and movable landing gear allowed for better control when landing.

This advertisement shows the popular Lambretta scooter from about 1950.

15

As tensions between the United States and USSR increased, the U.S. felt its duty was to defeat communism throughout the world. In 1947 President Harry S. Truman announced the Truman Doctrine, by which the U.S. pledged both financial and military support to Greece, which was experiencing a communist-led **civil war**, and Turkey, whose borders were threatened by Soviet expansion. Later, in 1957, President Dwight D. Eisenhower announced his own doctrine, which similarly promised aid to countries that resisted communism, this time in the Middle East.

India and Pakistan

The government in the United Kingdom recognized that it would be wrong to hold onto its empire in India, and so it began to plan for Indian independence. But this was not easy. About two-thirds of India's 400 million citizens were Hindu, while less than a third were Muslim. The two sides began to fight over who would rule after India gained its independence. One side or the other rejected every plan suggested by the United Kingdom. In August 1946 there were riots between Hindus and Muslims in Calcutta and Bengal, and 500 people were killed.

Two states

Faced with increasing violence that it could not stop, the British government announced in 1947 that it was leaving India. Talks between the United Kingdom and representatives of the two groups in India tried to find a way for the two communities to live together. These talks failed. The **Muslim League** demanded an independent Muslim country, and so the UK agreed to the creation of an entirely new country called Pakistan, made up of the regions where Muslims were the majority.

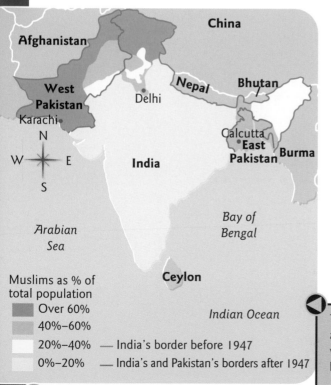

Muslims as % of total population
- Over 60%
- 40%–60%
- 20%–40% — India's border before 1947
- 0%–20% — India's and Pakistan's borders after 1947

The map shows the borders of India and Pakistan after an Act of Parliament was passed in 1947 that made them both independent countries.

New borders

In 1947, as soon as the Act of **Parliament** creating the two new countries was passed, millions of Muslims began fleeing from India into Pakistan. Similar numbers of Hindus fled in the opposite direction. About ten million people took part in this mass movement. In the chaos, about one million people were killed by **extremists** on both sides. Many of those killed were Sikhs, a religious minority in India that was given no country of its own.

Indian refugees crowd onto trains after the two new countries are created. Muslims flee to Pakistan and Hindus flee to India in one of the largest transfers of population in history.

Gandhi assassinated

Mahatma Gandhi was a very popular leader in India who had always had the support of both Hindus and Muslims. He wanted a single, independent country where all Indians could live in peace together. When the fighting broke out, he managed to calm the situation a little. He could do nothing, however, to stop the attacks of one side against the other. Then, in January 1948, a Hindu extremist, who was outraged at Gandhi's acceptance of other religions, shot him. Gandhi's **assassination** brought much of the fighting to an end, since both sides had greatly respected him. Although the fighting gradually stopped, the tensions between the two countries remained.

Israel and the Middle East

People in the Middle East were also demanding their independence from empires. The United Kingdom and France, countries that controlled parts of the region, accepted the demands of **nationalist** groups, and new countries such as Syria and Lebanon gained their independence after the war. In Palestine the situation was more complicated. Palestine was under British rule, but there were two conflicting groups wanting independence within the country. The majority group of Arabs in Palestine wanted to create an independent Arab state. Palestine, however, also had a community of Jews who felt that they had a claim to a homeland in Palestine. Before Roman times, there had been a Jewish state in Palestine, which the Romans had conquered. Many Jews from all over the world believed that they had a right to take back that homeland.

Two promises

During World War I, the United Kingdom had needed help to defeat Turkey. At first, they had promised independence to Arab nationalists in return for their help in fighting the Turks. Later, for the same reason, they also promised to create a national home in Palestine for the Jews. Neither of these promises gave exact details, so both Arabs and Jews could claim the British had promised them the **territory** they wanted.

Starting in 1944, British forces in Palestine came under attack from Jewish groups demanding independence. After the war, large groups of Jewish immigrants wanted to settle in Palestine. Survivors of the Holocaust, they gained international sympathy.

Creation of Israel

The United Kingdom handed over the problem of Palestine to the United Nations in 1947. The UN came up with the idea of splitting Palestine between Arabs and Jews. On May 14, 1948, the country of Israel came into existence, while the city of Jerusalem remained under international control.

Unanswered questions

The British foreign minister made a statement to Parliament in 1947, posing questions that faced the UN:

"Shall the claims of the Jews be allowed, that Palestine is to be a Jewish country?
Shall the claims of the Arabs be allowed, that it is to be an Arab country?
Shall it be a Palestinian country where the interests of both communities are as carefully balanced and protected as possible?"

(FROM MASTERING WORLD HISTORY BY NORMAN LOWE)

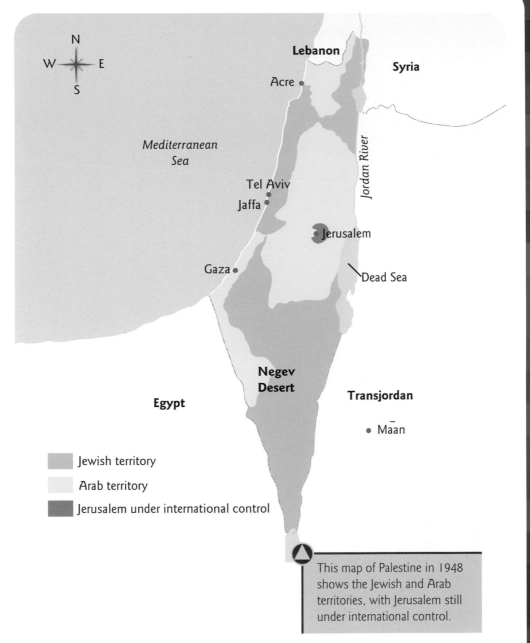

N
W —✶— E
S

Lebanon

Syria

Acre •

*Mediterranean
Sea*

Jordan River

Tel Aviv
Jaffa •

Jerusalem

Gaza •

Dead Sea

**Negev
Desert**

Egypt

Transjordan

• Maan

Jewish territory

Arab territory

Jerusalem under international control

This map of Palestine in 1948 shows the Jewish and Arab territories, with Jerusalem still under international control.

The 1948 War

The day after Israel came into existence, a war broke out as Arab armies from neighboring countries invaded and attacked Israel. Israel won the war and ended up with about three-quarters of Palestine—far more than the UN had set aside for it. The Palestinian Arabs ended up without a country or a homeland. Some were in the enlarged country of Israel, some in an area taken by Jordan, and hundreds of thousands were expelled by Israel. They became refugees in camps in neighboring Arab countries, where many still live today.

People's Republic of China

During World War II, nationalists in China fought against the Japanese, who had invaded their country. The nationalists were divided into a non-communist group and a communist group, which was led by Mao Zedong. Mao's army was more successful in winning the support of the country's **peasants**, but the non-communists felt stronger because of the support of the United States. The result, in 1945, was a civil war in China.

Civil war

The United States helped the non-communist forces take over regions of China that had been occupied by the Japanese. Mao's army, however, was better organized and the soldiers were more dedicated and loyal. Many of the leaders of the non-communist forces took money, given by the United States to help them fight their battles, and kept it for themselves. Mao was not **corrupt**, and his army had a strong belief in what it was fighting for. When the two armies met in battles, the non-communists often surrendered without resistance.

Mao's China

Mao and the communists won the civil war, and the People's **Republic** of China came into existence in October 1949. The defeated non-communist nationalists fled to the Chinese island of Taiwan, refusing to accept Mao's new China.

The invasion of China by Japan had started in 1937, and the twelve years of war had wrecked the Chinese economy. The tasks facing the communist government of a country of 600 million were enormous, but Mao managed to rebuild the country. Large amounts of land, once owned by wealthy landlords, were distributed to peasants.

Chairman Mao announces the founding of the People's Republic of China at Tiananmen Square, Peking (now Beijing), China, October 1949.

Western powers wondered how closely linked China and the USSR might become. They both had communist governments and they were both suspicious of the United States. Mao feared that the United States, which had supported the side that opposed him in the civil war, might try to plan a **counterrevolution** in China. While this brought China and the USSR together, Mao was also very determined to keep the new Chinese republic independent.

Tibet

Tibet had been part of the old Chinese Empire, but it was not part of China. When the communists took power in 1949, they were determined to regain control of Tibet. In 1950 Chinese forces invaded. Tibetan appeals to the West for help were ignored. In 1959 there was a rebellion against Chinese rule, but it was brutally crushed. The Tibetan leader, the Dalai Lama, went into **exile** in India.

Chinese troops march over the highlands toward the Tibetan frontier after their invasion of Tibet in 1950.

Growing threats

In the United States, the success of the communists in China was seen as a major defeat. China was rapidly becoming one of the world's great powers, and to have it ruled by communists was seen as a disaster. This news came at the same time as the first evidence that the USSR had atomic bombs. Both events triggered a review of the United States' defense policy. The United States had lost its power to threaten the USSR with the atomic bomb if the USSR could now do the same. The review recommended increasing spending on non-nuclear weapons from $13 billion to $50 billion.

War in Southeast Asia

Before World War II, Vietnam had been part of the French Empire in Asia. When the war ended, the Vietnamese wanted their independence, but France refused. In 1945 Ho Chi Minh, the Vietnamese leader, declared Vietnam independent. He led a group of nationalists that attacked the French in what became a nine-year struggle for independence. Because Ho Chi Minh was a communist, France and the United States saw Vietnam's struggle for independence as a communist threat. In order to stop another communist country from emerging in Asia, the United States began to financially support the French side in the war against independence. At the same time, the newly communist China supplied Ho Chi Minh's nationalist forces with weapons. The war ended when the French were defeated at Dien Bien Phu in 1954.

French foreign legion soldiers capture and question a Vietnamese nationalist during the Vietnamese fight for independence, 1954.

Vietnam divided

After the French defeat, representatives of all the countries involved attended a peace conference. An agreement was reached, and Vietnam was divided into two halves by a line called the 17th parallel. Ho Chi Minh's forces controlled the north, while a government friendly to the United States controlled the south. This was to be a temporary arrangement until a general election could create a united country. Ho Chi Minh accepted the agreement because he was so confident about winning a national election.

The government in the south of Vietnam refused to take part in a general election. The United States did not stop this decision, fearing a communist victory. The resulting conflict gradually developed into a civil war, and the government in the south came to depend on money from the United States. U.S. citizens and leaders did not realize that supporting the government in the south of Vietnam would lead to the United States' involvement in the Vietnam War from 1954 to 1970.

The map shows Vietnam, after the division into North and South Vietnam in 1954; and Malaya, which gained independence from the United Kingdom in 1957.

China

Dien Bien Phu • Haiphong
Hanoi • •

Laos **North Vietnam**

----------- 17th parallel

Thailand

Cambodia **South Vietnam**

Phnom • Saigon
Penh

Malaya

N
W ✛ E
S

War in Malaya

The country of Malaya in Southeast Asia was part of the British Empire. Here, too, there was a demand for independence after World War II. Malaya had a large Chinese population, and Chinese communists fought the British before being defeated in the early 1950s. The British began to move the Chinese villagers they suspected of helping the communists into specially guarded villages. At the same time, independence was promised in the future. The Malay population accepted this and did not support the rebels. In 1957 Malaya gained independence, later renaming itself Malaysia.

Climbing Mount Everest

While wars were dividing Vietnam and Malaya, two men were climbing the highest mountain in the world, Nepal's Mount Everest, and celebrating **internationalism** when they reached the top. New Zealander Edmund Hillary and his guide from Nepal, Tensing Norgay, reached the top at 29,028 feet (8,848 meters) above sea level on May 29, 1953. Hillary described the final ascent:

Edmund Hillary and his guide, Tensing Norgay, make their historic final ascent to the summit of Mount Everest.

"It was a beautiful day with a moderate wind. As we got there, my companion threw his arms around me and embraced me. I took photographs of Tensing holding a string of flags— those of the United Nations, Britain, Nepal, and India."

THE COLD WAR

The term *Cold War* came to describe the period after 1945 when the United States and the USSR highly distrusted each other. They were the superpowers of the world, and they both tried to influence world affairs in ways that suited their very different ideas about society. Each side thought its economic system was the best. The United Kingdom, France, Italy, Canada, and seven other nations stood firmly on the side of the United States and joined the **North Atlantic Treaty Organization** (NATO), a military **alliance** formed in 1949. Six years later, the USSR formed its own military alliance with other countries, called the **Warsaw Pact**.

The cold war in Asia

Korea became the first casualty of the United States–USSR rivalry. In 1945 Korea (which had been occupied by the Japanese during the war) was **liberated** by Soviet and U.S. forces. The Soviet and U.S. liberators agreed to divide the country between a communist government in the north and a non-communist one in the south. In 1950 North Korea, probably with the backing of the new communist Chinese government, invaded the south in an attempt to unify the country. The United States responded by calling on the United Nations to oppose the invasion.

U.S. Air Force B29s drop their cargo of bombs on a strategic target during the Korean War, about 1950.

War in Korea

Troops, mostly from the United States, but from twenty countries in all, arrived in Korea. When these troops pushed into North Korea, China sent in its own forces to push them back. China's confidence in challenging the United States came as a shock to U.S. generals. They had no idea that China would be so ready to fight them. Some generals, including Douglas MacArthur, a commander in World War II, talked of using atomic bombs and invading China in order to crush the opposition in Korea. The war turned into a bitter conflict, and the U.S. Air Force dropped almost as many (non-atomic) bombs on North Korea as had been dropped on Germany in World War II.

The North Korean troops treated their prisoners of war very badly, with a third of them dying in the first winter of the war. In one prisoner of war camp, there was a rebellion, but it was put down with tanks. When a settlement was finally negotiated, the last sticking point was the release of prisoners of war. One of the problems was that two-thirds of the Chinese prisoners of war refused to return to China, where they would be forced into the Chinese army again.

The wastefulness of war

The Korean War lasted three years. At the end of it, the division between North and South Korea was exactly the same as it had been at the start. Four million Korean civilians and soldiers lost their lives, and five million people were left homeless. About a quarter of a million Chinese soldiers died. United States casualties were 54,000 dead and 100,000 wounded. Of the many other UN forces that took part in the war, about 3,000 died.

Korean refugees step through the devastated streets of Inchan, on the west coast of Korea, after a U.S. attack on the port, September 16, 1950.

Reds Under the Beds

The **propaganda** of the Cold War affected many aspects of life in the United States. Communism was seen as a kind of virus. The government began to be concerned that communist spies were in the United States, where they were finding out military secrets and passing them to the USSR. In 1951 engineer Julius Rosenberg and his wife, Ethel, were found guilty of selling secrets to the Soviets. They were sentenced to death and were later executed in New York in 1953, even though there were calls for mercy from all over the world.

Joseph McCarthy

Joseph McCarthy was a Republican senator who was not well known in U.S. politics. But in 1950 he announced that he had a list of over 200 people working in the **State Department** who were members of the American Communist Party. He never produced a list, or even evidence to support his claim, but he made many Americans fearful of a secret communist network. McCarthy began a campaign of accusing public figures, such as the playwright Arthur Miller, of being communists. He gained the support of many national newspapers and politicians.

Screenwriter Dalton Trumbo, one of the Hollywood celebrities accused of having links to communism, angrily leaves the witness stand on October 28, 1947.

26

Un-American activities

In 1952 McCarthy was made head of a committee charged with investigating the loyalty of government employees. Eventually all sorts of people were accused of "un-American activities," even though many of them had done nothing wrong. Many of those being accused by McCarthy were Hollywood directors and screenwriters. The committee accused government employees, clergymen, lawyers, writers, and even an army general. Thousands of wrongly accused people lost their jobs as a result of McCarthy's accusations: 9,500 civil servants, 600 teachers, and hundreds of actors, writers, and performers. Of those that were accused, 400 went to jail. Some people protested that McCarthy was in danger of damaging freedom of speech. Humphrey Bogart and Lauren Bacall, two very famous movie stars, took part in a demonstration in Washington DC against what was happening.

A group of Hollywood celebrities, including Lauren Bacall, demonstrate against Senator McCarthy outside the Capitol Building, Washington DC, October 1947.

In June 1953 the hearings led by McCarthy were broadcast on television. When the public watched ordinary-looking people being accused and harassed by the senator, they began to turn against the hunt for communists. McCarthy was replaced as head of the committee in 1954 and was criticized by the Senate later that same year. The search for communist sympathizers continued, however, and in 1954 a law was passed making the Communist party illegal.

Reds under the beds

A popular joke term to describe the period of Senator McCarthy's investigation was "reds under the beds." It described the atmosphere of fear in the United States during those years, when people were worried that communist spies might be bugging their homes or even hiding under their beds. The word *reds* came from the fact that the color red was always the traditional color of the communist flag.

The Cold War in Space

The Cold War resulted in an **arms race** between the United States and the USSR, as both sides competed to produce better weapons. Since nuclear weapons were now the most powerful weapons possible, a race developed to see who could transport a nuclear bomb to an enemy target in the fastest possible time.

Sputnik

In 1957 the USSR launched *Sputnik,* the first **satellite** ever to leave Earth and orbit around it. Weighing only 184 pounds (83 kilograms), having a diameter of only 22 inches (56 centimeters), and carrying a radio transmitter, *Sputnik* was made to investigate outer space.

U.S. scientists saw the successful launch of *Sputnik* by the USSR as a terrible defeat. They felt that Soviet technology had shown itself to be better than U.S. technology. A famous scientist, Edward Teller, said on television that the United States had lost "a battle more important and greater than Pearl Harbor."

It took a powerful rocket to launch *Sputnik.* Such a rocket, it was feared, could be armed with a nuclear bomb and fired at the United States. A month later, *Sputnik II,* weighing half a ton (500 kilograms), was launched, this time with a dog named Laika inside. Sadly, Laika stopped barking during the flight and presumably died.

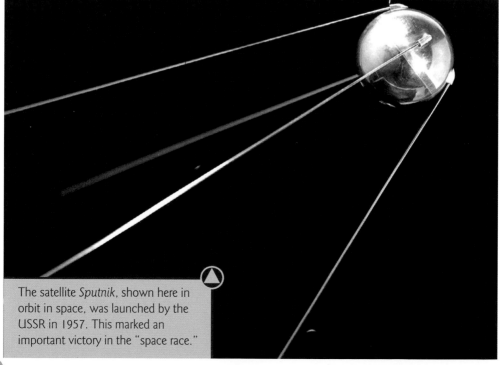

The satellite *Sputnik,* shown here in orbit in space, was launched by the USSR in 1957. This marked an important victory in the "space race."

Vanguard and Explorer

In December of the same year, in a glare of publicity, the United States launched a *Vanguard* satellite. At 3 pounds (1.4 kilograms), it was tiny compared to the successful Soviet ones. The attempt failed. The following January, the United States successfully launched *Explorer I*, and a series of U.S. satellites followed. The space race had begun. About three weeks after the USSR put the first man in space (see below), the U.S. began Project Mercury (1961–63), which was the country's first attempt at manned space flight. In 1962 John Glenn became the first American man in space.

The "space race"

As huge amounts of money went into the United State's space program, the National Aeronautics and Space Administration (NASA) was set up. The aim was always to be ahead of the USSR. One air force official, when asked what he expected to find on the Moon, replied "Russians." For other people, though, the space race was about mankind's natural interest in outer space.

The first man in space

On April 12, 1961, a Russian air force major, Yuri Alekseyevich Gagarin, became the first human to travel into space, aboard Earth satellite *Vostok I*. His journey was a single orbit of Earth, which lasted one hour and 48 minutes. He traveled at a speed of 17,000 miles (27,400 kilometers) per hour. Gagarin became world famous as the first man in space. He remained in the USSR air force as a test pilot, before being killed in a 1968 crash.

The Russian astronaut Yuri Gagarin awaits takeoff in his astronaut suit and helmet.

The life of baseball player Jackie Robinson in many ways embodied the civil rights struggles of the period. When he joined the Brooklyn Dodgers in 1947, Robinson became the first black player in major league baseball. He became Rookie of the Year and went on to win many honors. Despite his abilities, he had to deal with fans yelling racist insults, pitchers aiming for his head, and players refusing to play against him. Robinson persevered through such abuse, and the strong example he set helped open the door for other black players and also changed the minds of some white Americans. After retiring in 1957, Robinson became active in the civil rights cause.

New leaders

The year 1953 saw a change in leadership for the world's two superpowers, the United States and the USSR. Joseph Stalin had been ruling the USSR since 1928, and he had become a cruel **dictator**. He stopped any disagreements with his policies by imprisoning his political opponents, and huge numbers of people died as a result of his dictatorship. People suspected of not supporting the government were sent to labor camps or killed. Stalin died suddenly in 1953. He was eventually replaced by Nikita Khrushchev in 1956.

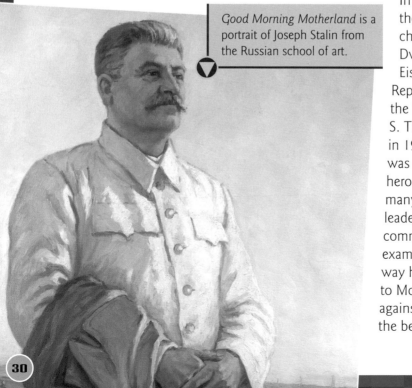

Good Morning Motherland is a portrait of Joseph Stalin from the Russian school of art.

In the United States there was also a change of leadership. Dwight D. Eisenhower, a Republican, replaced the Democrat Harry S. Truman as president in 1953. Eisenhower was a World War II hero and was seen by many as a practical leader who would use common sense. An example of this was the way he brought an end to McCarthy's campaign against "reds under the beds."

Eisenhower

Dwight D. Eisenhower was elected the 34th president of the United States in 1952. He had been the commander of the Allied powers during World War II and had commanded the invasion of Europe against Nazi Germany in 1944. While he was president, he kept the peace with the Soviet Union while building up U.S. nuclear weapons. He also began the United States' system of interstate highways. This made travel between one state and another far easier and changed the way that people lived, worked, and traveled. He died in 1969.

Dwight D. Eisenhower greets cheering crowds from the roof of his car during his 1952 presidential election campaign.

The Khrushchev era begins

Khrushchev publicly criticized Stalin's rule, pointing out to the Soviet public the cruelty of his policies and the way people had suffered as a result. After he took office, about eight million political prisoners were released from labor camps.

Khrushchev began a vast house-building program, encouraged the production of consumer goods, and allowed newspapers more freedom to report the news. He expanded the area of the Soviet Union's farmland by bringing previously **uncultivated** land into use. Khrushchev also put forward the idea that the USSR needed to have a peaceful relationship with the United States if nuclear war was to be avoided. It seemed as if a new and less aggressive relationship between the superpowers would now be possible.

Migration

In the postwar years, massive numbers of people migrated. Unsettled by the war and the political changes that followed it, they looked for new places to live. In 1948 the United States passed the Displaced Persons Act, which would eventually lead to hundreds of thousands of displaced Europeans entering the country. The United States also took in thousands of people from Mexico, Asia, and the West Indies.

In 1952 the McCarran-Walter Act was signed into law. It restricted the number of people who could immigrate from certain parts of the world—for example, it severely limited the number of Asians who could enter the U.S. Also, in line with the political atmosphere of the day, the act gave the government the power to resist entry to and deport immigrants who were perceived as a political—meaning a communist—threat.

In 1948 the United Kingdom passed a Nationality Act, which granted British citizenship to people of the **Commonwealth**. At first men came alone from Pakistan, India, and the Caribbean, often for low-paying jobs. Later, after they were settled, they brought their families to live with them. Immigrant groups formed small communities within the UK. Alongside the unskilled laborers came doctors, lawyers, and businessmen who were able to take up these professions in the UK.

The *Empire Windrush* arrives at Tilbury Docks, England, with 482 Jamaican immigrants on board, June 1948.

The Windrush generation

After the 1952 act in the U.S. restricted immigration there, the British began encouraging families from the West Indies to move to the United Kingdom, where there was a shortage of workers. The first ship bringing immigrant workers from the West Indies was the *Empire Windrush*, which docked in London in June 1948. The first generation of people who came to the UK after the war became known as the Windrush generation.

Discrimination

Immigrants found that life in the United Kingdom was not as pleasant as they might have thought. At work they were **discriminated** against, and they were not always welcome when they tried to find housing. It was not uncommon to find signs hanging in the windows of houses with rooms to rent saying "No Coloreds" or "No blacks or Irish." At the time, this was not illegal.

A black immigrant reads a sign on a British boardinghouse door that says: "Rooms to let—no colored men," September 1958.

Parliament began to discuss ways of making it illegal to discriminate against people because of their color or race. A law making racial discrimination illegal was not finally passed until the 1960s. In some London suburbs, there were riots against the settlement of black people in the area. In 1962 Parliament removed the automatic right of Commonwealth citizens to enter the UK freely, since they were becoming concerned about the threat of large-scale immigration.

Multicultural society

While times have often been quite hard for immigrants, whatever country they settled in, their arrival has always added something to their new home. Indeed, the history of the United States reflects a mix of cultures from around the world. Waves of immigration in the 1950s eventually brought new ideas in all areas of life, from food to music, theater, politics, medicine, religion, and much more.

Demanding Civil Rights

In the United States, African Americans began to demand the same civil rights as other United States citizens. About 10 percent of the U.S. population was black, and many of these people were the descendants of Africans who had been kidnapped and brought to the United States as slaves. In the 1950s, in some states, black citizens did not have many of the same rights and freedoms as white citizens. Even in states that did not discriminate, some white people thought of black people as their inferiors. In many southern states of the United States, black people could not vote, attend white schools or restaurants, or join **labor unions**. They did the poorest paid work and lived in the poorest conditions. In 1947 President Truman proposed a law to end discrimination, but Congress rejected the proposal.

As they had done before the war, black people began to challenge each act of discrimination in the courts. In one of these challenges, "Brown vs. Board of Education" in 1954, **segregation** in schools was declared illegal. All schools were ordered to accept both white and black students. This caused massive resistance among some white people in the South, where many would rather close down their schools than have black students attend.

In 1957, when the schools in Little Rock, Arkansas, were ordered to accept black students, white parents and the governor of the state, Orval Faubus, resisted. Faubus brought in the National Guard to stop black children from entering white schools. President Eisenhower responded by sending in 10,000 troops to enforce the law and protect black children as they attended school.

The U.S. Army is ordered by President Eisenhower to guard black students attending school in Little Rock, Arkansas, October 1957.

Rosa Parks

In Montgomery, Alabama, as in many towns in the South, black people had to give up their seat on a bus if a white person wanted it. In 1955 an African-American civil rights activist named Rosa Parks refused to give up her seat to a white man. She was arrested and convicted of disorderly conduct. She appealed the sentence, and eventually the U.S. Supreme Court ruled that segregation on buses was illegal. Her treatment began a year-long **boycott** by Montgomery's 50,000 black citizens, who refused to use the city's buses until they were desegregated. The boycott focused many people's minds on civil rights issues and made them realize that black people were prepared to take action in order to get equal rights.

The campaign for civil rights

Martin Luther King Jr. became the leader of the civil rights movement, leading **sit-ins** and demonstrations against segregation in the South. In many states, black people found it difficult to vote, either because they were intimidated at the polls or because local governments put in place unfair taxes or tests intended to prevent blacks from voting. The civil rights movement encouraged black people to register and supported those who were brave enough to do so.

Civil rights laws

In 1957 a law was passed that, among other things, set up an investigation into voting problems for blacks. This led, in 1960, to a new law that provided official help for black people wanting to register. Progress was being made, but there was still the problem of convincing some whites to accept the need for such laws.

Rosa Parks sits in the front of a bus in Montgomery, Alabama, after the successful boycott of the city's buses.

Martin Luther King Jr.

Martin Luther King Jr. was a prominent religious figure and one of the leaders of the civil rights movement. He taught people to take part in nonviolent protests and persuaded many white people to take up the cause of civil rights. He toured churches, where he preached and raised funds for the civil rights movement. Later, in the 1960s, he led bigger and bigger protests against segregation, many of which were met by police violence. He was imprisoned in 1963 in Birmingham, Alabama. Each peaceful demonstration drew more and more support for black civil rights. In 1964 he received the Nobel Prize for Peace. He was assassinated in 1968.

Demanding Self-Rule

In the years after World War II, nationalists in countries that had been ruled by an empire—including those of France, the United Kingdom, and the Netherlands—began demanding independence. The former empires dealt with the nationalists in various ways. Sometimes a peaceful agreement was reached. Other times, independence only came as a result of violent struggle.

Independence after violence

In the years after World War II, the nationalist majority in the east African state of Kenya, which was a British colony, wanted independence. The tiny minority of 66,000 white settlers in the country wanted it to remain a British colony. The white settlers wanted to start a conflict with the nationalists, in the hope that the United Kingdom would get involved and crush the nationalist movement. The whites would then be able to hold onto their power.

The white settlers got their wish in 1952, when a large group called the Mau Mau began a campaign of violence against them and the black people who worked for them. The Mau Mau came mainly from one tribe, the Kikuyu, which had lost much of its best land to white settlers. The United Kingdom sent in 100,000 troops. Over the next eight years of fighting, some 10,000 people, mostly Africans, were killed.

Mau Mau troops line up at a secret hideout in Meruland, Kenya, December 1963.

Although the Mau Mau were defeated, the United Kingdom came to realize that the desire for independence in Kenya was so strong that it would have to be granted. This happened in 1963. Algeria, in North Africa, also had to experience a long and painful war before France finally granted its independence in 1962.

Uprising in Hungary

It was not only the United Kingdom and France that faced demands for independence. After World War II, the USSR had built up its own empire in eastern Europe. Countries such as Poland, Romania, Bulgaria, and Hungary were ruled by communist governments that did what the powerful USSR asked.

The people of these eastern European countries did not like being told what to do by the USSR, and in the 1950s they began to stage political protests. In 1956 there was a serious challenge to Soviet rule by ordinary citizens in Hungary.

A new government came to power and promised to allow other parties to stand for elections.

The USSR was not going to let this happen. Soviet tanks and troops arrived in Hungary's capital, Budapest, and there was fighting in the streets. When the Russian troops had finally put down the uprising, 30,000 people had died. The USSR had made it clear that opposition would not be allowed.

Soviet tanks cross a Budapest street as they move in to crush the Hungarian uprising of October 1956.

New nations

This is a list of some of the nations that gained independence from European powers between 1945 and the early 1960s:

From the United Kingdom:
India and Pakistan (1947)
Malaya (1957)
Nigeria (1960)
Jamaica, Trinidad and Tobago (1962)
Northern Rhodesia (later called Zambia) (1964)

From the Netherlands:
East Indies (later called Indonesia) (1949)

From France:
Syria (1946)
Vietnam (1954)
Morocco and Tunisia (1956)
Algeria (1962)

From Italy:
Libya (1951)

From Belgium:
Congo (1961)

Cuba and Castro

At this time, Cuba was an independent republic, but U.S. companies owned half of the country's land and most of its important industries, such as sugar, tobacco, textiles, iron, nickel, and copper. What upset poor farmers and factory workers most was Fulgencio Batista, the corrupt dictator who seized power in 1952 and ruled every aspect of their lives.

Social problems

Batista did nothing to improve the lives of ordinary Cubans. Many of them depended on the sugar industry for work, but each year, when the harvest was over, unemployment reached 30 percent. There was no **welfare** system, and most people lived in poverty. Much of the country's wealth was going to U.S. companies and to a small class of wealthy Cubans.

Fidel Castro

Fidel Castro became a leading nationalist in Cuba. He wanted an end to Batista's corrupt government and a fairer distribution of land to peasants. At this stage, he was not a communist. When he began a **guerrilla war** in 1956 against Batista, his army was very small.

Batista tried to crush Castro and his guerrilla army, but he was not successful. More Cubans supported Castro because of the brutality of the government. Because of this support, the United States, which had always supported the government, became unwilling to supply any more weapons to Batista's army and cut off its supplies. In January 1959 Batista fled from Cuba. Castro established a new government.

Fidel Castro waves to a crowd upon his arrival in Havana, Cuba, after Batista fled the country in January 1959.

Who was Che Guevara?

Che Guevara was born in Argentina and became a doctor, but later he joined Castro's guerrilla force in Cuba. He played an important part in forcing Batista to flee. He returned to South America in 1966 and joined another guerrilla movement in Bolivia. He was captured and killed there in October 1967. Images of Che Guevara became very popular in the 1960s and remain popular. Many perceived him as a hero, since much of his work aimed to represent the interests of the poor and powerless.

A market stall in Cuba sells the popular image of the communist revolutionary Che Guevara on brightly colored posters.

Castro and the United States

Relations between Cuba and the United States got much worse. Castro wanted to deal with the country's social problems, and his government took control of the island's U.S.-owned oil refineries. This annoyed the United States, which responded in 1960 by placing an **embargo** on all Cuban goods. More industries in Cuba were then taken over by the government, and Castro turned to the USSR for help in buying its products.

All this convinced the United States that Cuba had become a communist country, and so it helped Cuban exiles with plans to invade and overthrow Castro. Cuba began to depend more and more on the USSR for military support and protection. In this way, Cuba's situation became tied up with the Cold War.

By the late 1950s, the U.S. economy was thriving. There had been a **"baby boom"** from 1945 to about 1955, as young Americans, many of them veterans of World War II, were eager to start their own families. Many aspired to own a single-family home, and so people began to travel to the suburbs, where there was more land. One example of this trend was Levittown, New York. Developed between about 1946 and 1951, it was a completely pre-designed community featuring thousands of affordable, mass-produced homes as well as community buildings, playgrounds, and schools. Shopping malls also began to develop during this period, since the average American now had both a car and spending money.

Ideal Home   October, 1956

"So <u>this</u> is

High Fidelity ..."

HIGH FIDELITY SYSTEMS

This advertisement is for hi-fi systems, which brought high-quality sound to home stereo products in the 1950s.

New ideas

Since nuclear energy had first been used in 1942, scientists had been developing a way to use it to make electricity. In 1956 the world's first nuclear power station was opened at Calder Hall, in Cumbria, England. The United States quickly followed with a nuclear power station in 1957. By 1959 a more efficient type of nuclear generator was built in Scotland. The future seemed bright with this inexpensive and supposedly safe way of producing electricity. In the same year, the United States announced that it had developed a tiny atomic generator weighing 5 pounds (2.3 kilograms), which would be used to power equipment in its satellites.

Literature

In the aftermath of war, some European writers called existentialists, including Albert Camus and Jean-Paul Sartre, examined the very meaning of existence. Other writers, such as British author George Orwell (*Animal Farm*, 1945; *1984*, 1949) and U.S. author Joseph Heller (*Catch-22*, 1961), used **satire** to examine the horrors of war.

New theater

In the United States and Europe, the Theater of the Absurd removed concepts of drama, chronological plot, themes, and recognizable settings from plays. *Waiting for Godot* (1952), by an Irish playwright named Samuel Beckett, became world famous. The play is about two tramps wandering in a strange landscape, doing nothing except waiting for someone to come. In contrast, the American playwrights Tennessee Williams (*A Streetcar Named Desire*, 1947), Arthur Miller (*Death of a Salesman*, 1949), and Eugene O'Neill (*Long Day's Journey into Night*, 1956) used a more realistic style to highlight the fragility of their flawed characters. All was not sadness and gloom. The 1950s also saw large audiences flock to musicals such as *The King and I* (1951), *The Sound of Music* (1959), and *West Side Story* (1957).

Strontium 90

During the 1950s, nuclear weapons tests took place around the world. The United States tested its weapons in the Nevada Desert and the Pacific Ocean. In 1958 scientists at Columbia University in New York discovered that, as a result of the nuclear testing of the previous decade, the amount of radioactive strontium 90 in all the people that they tested had increased by 30 percent. Strontium 90 collects in human bone, and in large enough doses it can cause leukemia (a serious disease) and bone cancer.

A huge mushroom cloud shoots up into the sky above the Pacific Ocean during nuclear weapons testing in the 1950s.

The Teenager

Before the 1950s, young men and women had worn the same clothes, hairstyles, and shoes as their parents. There was little time or money for entertainment, or for enjoying being young. The 1950s saw a radical change. As the economies of the West boomed, teenagers had pocket money to spend on leisure activities.

Teenagers suddenly had enough money to go to the movies regularly. The entertainment industry realized that this was a valuable new market. Directors began to make movies aimed at young people such as *The Wild One* (1953), starring Marlon Brando as a leather-clad biker, or *The Blackboard Jungle* (1955), about a class of rebellious students. *Splendor in the Grass* (1961), starring Natalie Wood and Warren Beatty, took on the controversial theme of teen pregnancy. In literature, J.D. Salinger's *Catcher in the Rye* (1951), the tale of an alienated prep school student, captured the confusion and angst of many teenagers of the period. Magazines aimed at teenagers sprang up with photos and articles about music stars, fashion, and love stories. *Seventeen* magazine, aimed specifically at teengage girls, began in 1944. Soda fountains, places where food and soft drinks were served, became a popular place for young people to meet. Here, teenagers could talk with friends and listen to the newest hit music on the jukebox.

Rocking and rolling

After 1955 teenagers had their own fashions and dances. Girls began to wear tight sweaters, full knee-length skirts called poodle skirts, flat shoes, and white socks instead of stockings. They often wore their hair in a ponytail. Boys wore checked shirts, leather jackets, jeans, and T-shirts. The most popular haircuts for boys were crew cuts or flattops. Popular dances included the twist and watusi. As girls twisted and turned on the dance floor, their skirts flared out and their ponytails bounced.

A teenage girl selects a song from the jukebox in a soda fountain in Manila, Philippines, about 1956.

James Dean

The clothes that teenagers wore and the music they listened to shocked and outraged the older generation. A few figures seemed to sum up this sense of rebellion. One of these was James Dean, a young actor whose movie roles, especially in *Rebel Without a Cause,* came to represent the stresses of being young. He was nominated for two Oscars, but died in a car crash at the age of 24. His tragic death at such a young age made him a legend.

Rebel Without a Cause, the popular teenage movie starring James Dean and Natalie Wood, was filmed in 1955.

Rock and Roll

Before World War II, music played and listened to by black people had a major impact on the music scene. Jazz music was very popular in the 1920s, and swing music developed out of this to great acclaim in the 1930s and 1940s. By the 1950s, however, jazz was popular mostly with a group of intellectual young people known as "beatniks," but not with the majority of people. Great musicians such as Charlie Parker, Thelonious Monk, Billie Holiday, and Miles Davis performed in clubs in New York to a loyal but relatively small group of fans.

After the war, another style of black music called R&B (rhythm and blues) began to be played on the radio stations that young white people listened to. This style used elements of southern blues and gospel. Record companies began to produce versions of R&B tunes sung and played by white artists. In 1951 the radio deejay Alan Freed referred to this new style as rock and roll, and a new phenomenon was born.

The first rock and roll song is widely believed to be "That's All Right Mama" by Elvis Presley, released in 1954. However, this is still debated. Some think rock and roll started as early as 1951, with "Rocket 88" by Jackie Bentson.

Rock and roll singer Elvis Presley performs "Hillbilly Heartbreak" onstage in Hollywood, California, June 22, 1956.

Regardless of when it started, the sound quickly became popular. Bill Haley and the Comets' hits "Shake Rattle and Roll" (1954) and "Rock Around the Clock" (1955) quickly climbed up the popular music charts. Black R&B artists Chuck Berry, whose hits included "Roll over Beethoven" (1956) and "Johnny B. Goode" (1958), and Little Richard, who was known for his stage show, were played alongside white artists such as Buddy Holly and Jerry Lee Lewis, whose music was more influenced by country.

The biggest rock and roll sensation of the 1950s was Elvis Presley. His singing style was a mixture of the music of southern blacks and the new teenage rebelliousness. As he sang, he danced in a way that no white performer had ever done before. He was good-looking and seemed like the boy no parent wanted their daughter to go out with—and so, of course, girls loved him! He wore his hair long (compared to the crewcuts of the time) and slicked back, with long sideburns; this was the style of street gangs, not teenagers.

The medium of television brought these acts into American living rooms. When Presley performed on the popular *Ed Sullivan Show* in 1957, the cameras had to film him from the waist up, so as not to shock Americans with the sight of Presley's swiveling hips.

Chuck Berry was one of the most popular US rock and roll stars of the 1950s.

Elvis cuts his hair

By 1958 Elvis was a rock star and a movie star, but his career came to a temporary end when he was **conscripted** into the U.S. Army in 1958. His manager, Colonel Parker, made the event into a publicity stunt, having Elvis filmed as he got an army crew cut. When he emerged two years later, Elvis was clean-cut and his songs were smoother. He concentrated on his movie career, making an album for each movie, often full of ballads. He became popular with adults as well as teens.

DANGEROUS TIMES

The United States and USSR were engaged in a rapidly increasing arms race throughout the postwar period. After dropping atomic bombs on Japan at the end of World War II, the United States had tested larger bombs. By 1949 the Soviets had also mastered nuclear technology. Given this threat, the United States sought an even more powerful weapon. Scientists developed the thermonuclear, or hydrogen, bomb – a weapon with far greater destructive power than anything before it.

A sense of nervousness was felt by all Americans. At schools, children practiced drills in which they had to "duck-and-cover" in the event of a nuclear attack. Some Americans even went so far as to build bomb shelters in their backyards, complete with food and other essentials.

Spy plane shot down

A meeting between the Soviet, U.S., British, and French leaders was due to take place in Paris in May 1960. The Soviet leader, Khrushchev, spoke of an "optimistic" mood for the chances of world peace. Suddenly, just before the conference was to begin, Khrushchev announced that a U.S. spy plane had been shot down over Soviet territory. The pilot, Gary Powers, had parachuted out and was arrested after landing safely.

U.S. Air Force pilot Gary Powers prepares to board a jet. His spy plane was shot down over the USSR in May 1960.

Bad feelings

The shooting down of the spy plane made the bad feelings of the Cold War begin to rise to the surface once more. Khrushchev arrived at the conference in Paris demanding an apology from the United States for sending spy planes over the USSR. President Eisenhower refused to do so, and so the Soviet leader stormed out of the conference. The Cold War was up and running once again.

Ban the bomb

Given the atmosphere of fear generated by McCarthy's hunt for communists, many Americans chose not to engage openly in politics during the postwar period. Others, however, decided to speak out against the threat posed by nuclear weapons. In 1957 a group called the National Committee for a Sane Nuclear Policy was formed in a bid to reduce the world's nuclear weapons, while college students across the country formed the Student Peace Union in 1959. These groups led protests and marches similar to those in the United Kingdom.

In 1955 scientist Albert Einstein and 51 other Nobel Prize winners warned of the dangers of the nuclear arms race. Later, over 9,000 scientists urged the United Nations to prevent nuclear testing.

Nuclear protesters carry out a sit-in outside Whitehall, London, United Kingdom, on February 18, 1961.

What happened to Gary Powers?

Gary Powers, the pilot of the spy plane, was put on trial in Moscow in August 1960. He pleaded guilty to spying, admitting that he had been illegally flying over the USSR. Pictures of Soviet airfields were found in his crashed plane. Powers was sentenced to ten years in prison, but was released two years later when he was exchanged for a Soviet spy caught by the United States.

The Berlin Wall

One city, two systems

Even though Berlin was a city in East Germany, the half of the country that was under Soviet control, the city itself was divided into two halves. One half was being run by the communist government of East Germany, and the other was run by the pro-United States West German government. Germans could move freely between the two parts of the city: the western part, under U.S., French, and British influence, and the eastern part, under Soviet influence.

This was causing a problem for East Germany because, since 1945, about two million of its citizens had chosen to go and live in West Germany, which was wealthier. Although the border between East and West Germany had been closed since 1952, they could travel to East Berlin and freely cross into the western part of the city. Once there, the government helped them reach West Germany using the protected air route that connected West Berlin with West Germany.

Brain drain

Over the first six months of 1961, the number of East Germans leaving through Berlin was rapidly increasing. Nearly 20,000 had left in March alone, and the country's economy was being affected. Many of those leaving were professionals and skilled workers, who left behind jobs that could not be easily or quickly filled.

East German soldiers build the Berlin Wall even higher to separate East and West Berlin, October 1, 1961.

Building the Wall

On August 12, 1961, Berliners started to hear news about a barrier of barbed wire being built across their city by the East German authorities. In the days that followed, the barbed wire was replaced by concrete blocks, and eventually a solid wall divided the two parts of the city. Some people's homes stood inside East Berlin, but their front doors opened into West Berlin. The army blocked up the doors, but people escaped through their windows. In June 1962 a man trying to cross the wall was shot and killed by an East German guard. Another 191 people would die trying to escape from East Berlin before the wall finally came down in 1989.

The Berlin Wall became a symbol of the world that the postwar decade had made. The world had become divided, like Berlin, into two halves, opposed to each other and with the capability of wiping each other out. It would be almost 30 years before the wall was no longer needed. The decade had seen huge changes in technology, and for Westerners at least there was a better quality of life. The term *teenager* had been born, and so had rock and roll. Television and movies had become everyday forms of entertainment. Cars got bigger and radios got smaller. It was an exciting time to be alive.

Only a white line

Before the Berlin Wall was built, the boundary between the two halves of the city was sometimes only a white line painted on a road. Each of the two halves of the city had its own police force, its own army, and its own currency. At the same time, though, buses and trains followed their traditional routes across the city. So, too, did the city's telephone lines. When the wall was built, people would stand on ladders to wave to their relatives who lived on the other side.

East German police carry eighteen-year-old Peter Fechter's lifeless body. He was shot by communists while trying to escape to the West on September 17, 1962.

TIMELINE

1945

The United Nations is formed
Harry S. Truman becomes president
Korea is divided into two states

1946

In Nuremberg, Germany, Nazi
leaders are tried and convicted of
war crimes

1947

The Marshall Plan to help European
countries rebuild their economies
is established
Dior launches the "New Look"
Civil war in China
Country of Pakistan is created
Winston Churchill first coins the
expression "the Iron Curtain"

1948

Blockade of West Berlin begins
Country of Israel is established

1949

USSR develops nuclear weapons
The United States passes a law
restricting entry to communists
The People's Republic of China
is established

1950

North Korea invades South Korea
China invades Tibet
The new Studebaker is put on sale

1951

The Rosenbergs are sentenced
to death in the United States
Joseph McCarthy begins his search
for communists

1952

Peace settlement in Korea
Coronation of the the British queen

1953

McCarthy hearings televised
Dwight D. Eisenhower is president
Death of Joseph Stalin

1954

The U.S. Supreme Court hears the
Brown vs. Board of Education
case
French defeated at Dien Bien Phu

1955

Rosa Parks case in the courts

1956

Hungarian uprising
World's first nuclear power station
is opened

1957

Boeing 707 jet airliner comes
    into service
Malaya gains its independence
Sputnik 1 is launched
Civil rights dispute in Little Rock,
    Arkansas, leads to civil rights law

1958

Quiz show scandals
U.S. Supreme Court says that Little
    Rock schools must integrate

1959

Alaska and Hawaii become the
    49th and 50th states
Rebellion in Tibet is crushed

1960

United States has 50 million
    television sets
John F. Kennedy is elected president

1961

Yuri Gagarin, a Russian, is the first
    person in space

1962

Algeria gains its independence
John Glenn is the first American
    in space

1963

Kenya gains its independence

FURTHER INFORMATION

Books

Brubaker, Paul. *The Cuban Missile Crisis in American History.* Berkeley Heights, NJ: Enslow, 2001.

Cole, Michael D. *John Glenn: Astronaut and Senator.* Berkeley Heights, NJ: Enslow, 2000.

Cox, Vicki. *Fidel Castro.* New York: Chelsea House Publishers, 2004.

Dornfeld, Margaret. *The Turning Tide: From the Desegregation of the Armed Forces to the Montgomery Bus Boycott.* New York: Chelsea House Publishers, 1995.

Downing, David. *Leading Lives: Martin Luther King.* Chicago: Heinemann Library, 2002.

Gaff, Jackie. *20th Century Music: The 40s & 50s: From War to Peace.* Chicago: Heinemann Library, 2002.

Jones, Helen. *20th Century Design: The 40s & 50s: War and Post War Years.* Chicago: Heinemann Library, 2000.

Levine, Ellen. *Freedom's Children: Young Civil Rights Activists Tell Their Own Stories.* New York: Puffin Books, 2000.

McNeese, Tim. *The Space Race.* New York: Children's Press, 2003.

Parker, Steve. *20th Century Media: The 1940s & 50s: The Power of Propaganda.* Chicago: Heinemann Library, 2003.

Reynolds, Helen. *20th Century Fashion: The 40s & 50s: Utility to New Look.* Chicago: Heinemann Library, 1999.

Shirley, David. *The History of Rock and Roll.* New York: Franklin Watts, 1999.

Simon, Scott. *Jackie Robinson and the Integration of Baseball.* Hoboken, NJ: Wiley, 2002.

Steele, Philip. *Leading Lives: Ho Chi Minh.* Chicago: Heinemann Library, 2003.

Taylor, David. *The Cold War.* Chicago: Heinemann Library, 2001.

Van Steenwyk, Elizabeth. *Dwight David Eisenhower, President.* New York: Walker & Company, 1987.

The mid-1940s to the early 1960s

Art	• Painter Jackson Pollock leads the abstract expressionism movement in art
Books and literature	• Anti-establishment authors called the Beat Generation include the author Jack Kerouac and the poet Allen Ginsberg • Science fiction becomes more popular with the actual possibility of space travel. Popular authors include Isaac Asimov and Ray Bradbury. • Harper Lee's *To Kill a Mockingbird* (1960)
Education	• Elizabeth Eckford is the first African-American teenager to enter the all-white Little Rock Central High School, Arkansas, in 1957
Fads and fashions	• Mattel introduces the Barbie doll in 1959 • The Hula-Hoop is introduced in 1958; 24 million sell in just two months
Music, film, and theater	• Director Alfred Hitchcock creates a series of popular thrillers, including *Psycho* (1960)
Scientific events	• Scientist Alfred Kinsey publishes a controversial report on male sexuality in 1948 • Scientists James Watson and Francis Crick discover the structure of **DNA** in 1953 • Scientist Jonas Salk's **polio** vaccine is available in 1955

GLOSSARY

alliance military or social agreement between two or more countries

Allied powers countries at war against Germany, Japan, and their supporters in World War II

arms race competition between countries to have more powerful weapons

assassinate to deliberately target and kill someone

atomic bomb weapon of mass destruction that releases an atom's energy

baby boom period between 1945 and about 1955 when the birth rate increased

Berlin Wall long barrier built to divide East and West Berlin

blockade method used to prevent something from happening

boycott refusing to have anything to do with a person or a group as a form of protest

capitalist someone who believes in an economy based on private ownership and profit

civilian person who is not a soldier or involved in war

civil rights essential rights of all citizens

civil war war taking place within a country, not against a foreign country

Cold War period of hostility between the United States and the USSR that existed from 1945 until the late 1980s

colony country ruled over by another country as part of an empire

Commonwealth group of countries once part of the British Empire

communist person who believes in government control of most aspects of life and spreading wealth

concentration camp prison camp where people are forced to live, usually under horrible conditions

conscripted called up into the military

consumer goods things that ordinary people need or want to buy

corrupt not honest

counterrevolution second revolution after a first one has failed

democratic country in which the people choose their leaders by voting

deported expelled from a country or region

detention camps places where people are kept, against their will, until a decision has been made about their future

dictator ruler with all the power

discriminate to make a judgment or choice on the basis of, for example, race or religion

displaced person name given to the thousands of people who ended up in the wrong country at the end of World War II

DNA tiny building blocks that are the basis of the characteristics we inherit from our parents

economy matters to do with money

embargo ban on trade of something with another country

empire control of other countries by a dominant power

ethnic minority small group with its own identity

exile expelled from one's own country, usually for political reasons

extremist person or political group that holds very strong views

Great Depression period after 1929 when industries all over the world went out of business and millions of people were unemployed

guerrilla war form of fighting against larger and more powerful forces that avoids an open battle

gulag harsh labor camp

Holocaust mass murder of European Jews and other ethnic groups by the Nazis during World War II

immigrant person who travels to another country to live there

internationalism policy of cooperation between countries

labor union organization formed by workers to protect their interests

liberate set free

Muslim League Indian political organization created in 1906 to protect the rights of Muslims in India

nationalist someone with a stong belief in the value of the nation to which he or she belongs

North Atlantic Treaty Organization (NATO) defense organization whose members were Canada, Denmark, France, Iceland, Italy, Luxembourg, the Netherlands, Norway, Portugal, the United Kingdom, and the United States. Greece and Turkey were admitted in 1952 and West Germany in 1955.

nuclear related to the energy of an atom, the tiny building block of all matter

parliament place where politicians make decisions and pass laws

peasant poor person who works on the land

polio virus that can lead to paralysis

propaganda information that presents only one point of view

rationed restricting the supply of scarce items, so that each person receives only a small amount

refugee person who has no home

republic form of government without a king or queen

satellite man-made object that orbits (circles) the Sun, Moon, or Earth

satire style of literature that examines and ridicules human behavior

segregation separating people based on differences such as race

sit-in form of political protest in which large numbers of protestors refuse to leave a building or area, making it unusable

Soviet having to do with the USSR

State Department government department in the United States dealing with domestic matters

territory land belonging to someone

thermoplastic material that gets soft when it is heated

transistor small semiconductor that is used as a circuit in electrical equipment

uncultivated farmland that has been not been used

United Nations international organization of countries. Its role is to achieve international cooperation in solving economic, social, cultural, or humanitarian problems.

USSR Union of Soviet Socialist Republics, a communist state dominated by Russia that disbanded in 1991

Warsaw Pact military alliance of seven European Communist nations, signed in 1955 and dominated by the USSR

welfare government-run program to help the poorer members of a country

INDEX